TABLE OF CONTENTS

PREFACE

If you run from your fears, they will follow you.
If you run straight at your fears, they will get out
of your way. **- Jen Sincero**

You're probably wondering, "How did we get here?"
Let's go back, not too far back, but back enough, to April 2019.
The day that changed my life forever. The past three years have
been a journey to say the least, and in these moments I felt hidden. No one knew who I was, no one knew what I was doing,
and no one was ready for how I was about to make my mark on
the world. To make a long story short, I'm Dr. Kelsei LeAnn.
I'm a licensed therapist that specializes in helping women
(although I do help some men) with mental health, childhood
trauma, and regaining self-love.

You're probably looking at the title of this book wondering where you fit in with all this. Let me break down what this
means. You see two couches side by side, one is clean and looks
brand new, and the other one is busted up. That is a visual representation of your life. Everything you have experienced is that
busted up couch, and before you experienced it you were perfectly fine, now you have all this trauma that's leaking out onto
everyone else. This is "The You Effect." Who you are affects
everyone around you. What you do changes everyone and ev-

erything about you. Not to mention, where you are now effects where you will go in the future. Everything ends with you. It's your job to take control. The goal of this book is to help you understand that you're not alone, you're not crazy, and you're not worthless.

In reality, you were created for such a time as this. This book is not one of those "feel good" tickle your ear type of books. This book will not always feel good to read, but in reality, healing doesn't always feel good. This is a raw and real conversation between you and me. We'll laugh together, cry together, scream together, get mad together, get sad together, but most importantly we will heal together. Page by page, chapter by chapter, we'll begin to confront our greatest fears and start unpacking some of our deepest trauma together. If you are reading this book, you are in one of three places. You're either at rock bottom after trying everything else, in the middle of a storm looking for a way to navigate through it, or you know if you don't find shelter soon the storm is going to overtake you.

Wherever you are in your journey, I want you to know that I see you.

You are not reading this by mistake. Everything in your life was crafted to bring you to this very moment. So grab a glass of wine, some tissues, and a highlighter. Get ready, because now you're in for the journey of your life.

WHAT IS CHILDHOOD TRAUMA?

This is not you. This is something moving through
you. It can leave out of the same door it came in.
- Cleo Wade

Before we can get into what childhood trauma is, let's first define it. Trauma, according to the International Society for Traumatic Stress Studies, is described as negative events that are emotionally painful in a way that overwhelms a person's ability to cope. Trauma can present itself in different ways. It can be mental, physical, or emotional. I get this question a lot: "Well Dr. K, what if my childhood wasn't that bad?" That's perfectly fine! Childhood trauma does not mean you had bad parents. It's more than that. Later on in the book, we'll discuss how parents can unconsciously pass down their unhealed trauma to their kids. Childhood trauma signifies that as children, we had high expectations and in some form or fashion we were let down. Fast forward to adulthood, we have the ability to not only change our stories, but to renew, relearn, and repower our minds and our lives. Having a parent constantly yelling and belittling you can be trauma. Growing up in the hood and wondering what you're going to eat tomorrow can be traumatic. Your

pain tolerance and your mental capacity determine your level of trauma.

Childhood trauma can take away your sense of security and well-being.

As a child, you expect your parents to protect you, to steer you in the right direction, and to come to your defense. Our parents are our heroes and when we see them hang up their capes we lose our sense of hope that they can save us. You learn your behavior and your feelings from your parent or guardian, and learning how to navigate through the ups and downs of life is a vital part of the developmental process. Children who experience any level or kind of trauma get stuck in the developmental process. This means repeated or single experiences that you may have been exposed to as a child that triggers your brain to go into survival mode. When you are exposed to trauma unconsciously, your brain automatically puts a wall up where the trauma occurred to protect you from it happening again.

I want you to imagine a construction site. On this site, workers are building a wall. While the workers are building this wall, people keep walking up to throw rocks, trying to knock the wall down as the workers are building. As you can imagine, these workers are frustrated that people keep throwing rocks, trying to destroy their work. That's what your mind is going through when you experience trauma. Immediately after the trauma, the workers in your mind start building a wall. Your

triggers, or even people who truly care about you, are trying to break through that wall (this is deeply frustrating you, the worker) which causes you to build up a wall, not allowing people to come in.

IDENTIFYING CHILDHOOD TRAUMA

It's not who you are that holds you
back, it's who you think you are not.
*- **Denis Waitley***

When it comes to childhood trauma, it is evident there are tons of signs for you to notice within yourself. One of the biggest signs of childhood trauma is being emotionally unstable. As children, our feelings are learned behavior. You're still learning and developing based on what your parents teach you about the basics. When you're a toddler, you're in the exploration stage where your parents will tell you to not touch the stove because it's hot, or to not play with plugs because you could hurt yourself. That is a reflection of learned behavior. Now, what's the difference between your feelings and your emotions?

As we just read, your feelings are learned behaviors while your emotions amplify the behavior you've learned. Let's imagine a fire. Your feelings are the fire already burning, and your emotions are the gasoline that makes the flame burn brighter. Your emotions escalate your feelings. They go hand in hand, but they are very different. That's why being emotionally unstable is a sign of childhood trauma. Your parents are sup-

posed to show you how to properly manage your feelings and emotions. This is often why you feel as if people never understand your feelings. You feel dismissed often and thrown all over the place emotionally.

You can also get facts and feelings mixed up, which is common when you're emotionally immature or underdeveloped. When you come upon a situation, I want you to analyze the facts of the situation. What are the facts?

Facts are the truth you can't negotiate with.

Think back on situations that you've faced that left you feeling a type of way emotionally. I want you to think about what's true about the situation. Did they lie? Cheat? Manipulate? That's the truth. What you feel about the truth is different. Not only are your facts and feeling mixed up, but if you look back at your past relationships you'll notice that most of them were toxic. Since you are a product of your experiences and your environment, if as a child all you saw growing up were toxic relationships, you tend to reflect that as you become an adult. Women especially try hard to avoid a relationship like the one they saw their parents have, yet unconsciously project their fears which allows narcissistic men to sense it and use it to their advantage.

When we are children, we're not taught to trust our voice. This causes us to be codependent, seeking validation before we can make a decision for ourselves. Confidence is key. Your lev-

el of confidence comes from your parents, and your reassurance does too. Confidence is defined as the feeling or belief that you can rely on someone or something with a firm trust. If you had an inconsistent or absent parent, it will affect your confidence. How confident you are as an adult is a direct reflection of how confident your parents raised you to be. Analyzing your beliefs, strengths, and capability, indicates a lack of confidence. I want you to reflect on where you heard or felt your incapability to do or be something. Where did the disqualification that you feel come from? Who taught you to think like that? If you recognize toxic traits inside of you as an adult, then they were there as a child. Reassurance on the other hand, is the action of removing one's doubts or fears. This is why reassurance and confidence go together. If you're not secure in something then the fear is still there.

Somewhere along the way your security got breached and you started to doubt yourself. Childhood trauma keeps you stuck on the hamster wheel of "what if's." If you're stuck in the past or future, this is a direct result of running away from your problems as a child or consuming yourself with something to get your mind off of your problems. This can cause you to be in a constant loop of a depressive state, experiencing anxiety, or even as far as suicidal ideations. Feeling like this can cause you to think that your voice has no power, and feel completely misunderstood. Due to you feeling misunderstood, you tend to feel responsible for other people's feelings, emotions, and their well-being. It can be described as being compelled to be there for people because you didn't have anyone there for you. You

don't want anyone to go through the pain that you experienced so you overextend yourself to please others. When our family doesn't talk about their own trauma or ever work through it, we begin to see generational trauma. When your great-grand-ma doesn't discuss what happened in 1922 between her and great-grandad, then generational trauma runs rampant in our lives. What our ancestors failed to realize is that as children we can sense pain and fear. We can see how dramatic and painful trauma truly is, and the emotions attached to it. We become emotional dumpsters for everyone else's life but fail to take out our own trash. This is your chance to be free.

Before you move on, let's review what was covered. Understanding trauma is the foundation for this book and I want you to start strong.
1. *Trauma is anything that overwhelms your ability to cope.*
2. *Trauma can show up mentally, emotionally or physically.*
3. *Trauma is the reason why you have so many walls built up. Your brain is trying to protect itself from going back to the original point where you security was breached.*

HOW CHILDHOOD TRAUMA AFFECTS YOUR ADULT RELATIONSHIPS

We have the power to restrengthen, recover and renormalize our brain even when it has suffered major trauma **- Dr. Caroline Leaf**

According to the National Child Traumatic Stress Network, 78 percent of children reported more than one traumatic experience before the age of five, 28 percent of children before the age of six had begun receiving treatment for traumatic experiences, including sexual abuse, neglect, exposure to domestic violence, and losing a loved one. When you're an adult you can develop what is called, complex post-traumatic stress disorder, which is characterized by difficulties in emotional regulation, memory, and self-perception.

As a child your identity begins to form. When you experience a traumatic childhood, you often experience memory loss. With this kind of trauma, you may have felt like something was always missing, but you didn't quite know what it was. This is why you can often disconnect from the important parts of yourself, even the people around you in order to survive. You tend to attract people who fit your traumatic identity and un-

consciously try to attract those who treat you wrong. You may be attracted to the wrong type of people and end up with people who aren't the best option for you. It can lead to a repetition of the past. You may end up over-extending yourself to people who are emotionally unavailable, narcissistic, or abusive.

This can lead you to believe that you're not worthy of any relationship and are better off alone. When you have negative experiences with relationships, you naturally tend to isolate yourself and become distant. This can begin as soon as the trauma is exposed or later on down the line, but healthy relationships with other people are crucial to personal development.

You may also start overthinking and overanalyzing everything. When you overthink, your mind keeps you in a constant negative loop. It keeps you stuck on the "what ifs, why me, and what happens now" thoughts. Overthinking can jeopardize your physical health through hair loss, weight gain, and other more serious illnesses. First things first, you need to get into the habit of noticing when you're thinking too much. The best way to track your thoughts is an emotion journal. Flip over to the back of this book to begin your emotion journal. There, I want you to write down what you think and why you think it. This will help you confront the lies that overthinking tells you. I also want you to begin the process of challenging your negative thoughts. Write out what you're thinking and write down two positive things to combat the thought. If you believe that a job won't hire you, write down two reasons why you deserve the job. You want to start practicing active problem solving because you can only solve what you are in control of. Your thoughts,

behavior, emotions, and actions are the only factors you can control. Overthinking something you have no control over only hurts you. You have to begin to compartmentalize. If you want to think about something, give yourself three minutes to think about it, write it, cry it out, scream, or whatever works for you and after five minutes, gather yourself and move on. Overthinking all day every day is allowing you to stay in a constant emotionally toxic cycle.

Another way to combat overthinking, is to practice the art of living in the now. Our minds are always focused on either yesterday or tomorrow. We're either stressing about what we have to do tomorrow or depressed about all the things we didn't do yesterday. We're in a constant mental and emotional rollercoaster in our minds. So what does living in the now mean?

It means to be present, being focused on the moment and not being distracted about the past or the future.

It's being grounded and focused on the now. Am I saying to never focus on the past or the present? Of course not. You need the past to look over your mistakes and success, and you need a future to plan for. I'm saying don't get wrapped up in tomorrow and yesterday, that you neglect today. So how can you be in the now and stop worrying? You can begin to practice mindfulness and take full control of who you are today. You

need to breathe. I can't express how important breathing is. Stress causes labored breathing.

It's as easy as taking ten deep breaths from your diaphragm, and while you're breathing focus on actually breathing and not on what you're stressed about. You have to find your groove. Begin to make the most out of your time by synchronizing your day-to-day activities with being present. If you think about doing something, do it as soon as you think about it instead of waiting to do it until later. Accept the things you cannot change. It does not serve you to be worrying about what or who you cannot control. Accept what you can control and move forward. Living in the now is staying healthy and finding joy. It's cutting down on your panic attacks, worrying less and staying grounded.

Renewing your mind, regaining your confidence, and repowering your life is an on-going process. Reconnecting with yourself is not a quick fix. When you establish your long term goals and work toward them, what was once impossible becomes easily attainable. Working on yourself and your mindset is the first step.

This can be a lot to take in all at once. To make sure you remember all of the key points, lets go over the basics:

1. *Complex post-traumatic disorder is when you have difficulty in remembering the details of your trauma. Consciously you do not recall the trauma, but it remains to affect your present life.*

2. *One symptom of complex post-traumatic disorder is overthinking. Overthinking brings false imaginations and realities to mind. To combat this, have an emotional journal where you can navigate all of your thoughts in a logical way.*

3. *Live in the now! You can't change the past and you can't predict the future. All you have is today. Own it.*

DID YOUR CHILDHOOD TRAUMA CAUSE YOU TO DISASSOCIATE?

People start to heal the moment they are heard.
- Cherly Richardson

Another symptom of childhood trauma is dissociation. Dissociation is used as a coping mechanism when you have gone through a traumatic experience. This is when your brain automatically blocks out the experience to avoid feeling any pain or feeling any future pain associated with the trauma. When dissociation occurs, you detach yourself from reality. Imagine being physically present, but your mind and emotions are somewhere else. This is what happens when someone has triggered you. You tend to space out and have no recollection of what is going on or what just happened. This is why people say you have a wall built up. How do you heal from an experience that you don't talk about? What if your mind blocks out the trauma and you forget it even occurred? You need to speak more about it and be more mindful of where you are. The more you stay quiet about your experiences, the more you detach.

The more you detach from your relationships, the weaker they become.

If you never heal from your own traumatic experiences, the trauma you've faced will be the next phase of the generational cycle. To stop detaching and dissociation, I encourage you to start speaking up, start journaling, start living your truth (not your trama) and begin to rebuild the pieces of your life. You're not a victim you're a survivor. Now, flip to the back of this book to fill out the victim to victor worksheet and move on to the next chapter.

HAS CHILDHOOD TRAUMA CAUSED YOU TO BE AN EMOTIONAL EATER?

Self-discipline begins with the mastery of your thoughts. If you don't control what you think, you can't control what you do. **- Napoleon Hill**

Emotional eating is a common crutch many people who have suffered from childhood trauma use to feel better. Emotional eating refers to the consumption of food to lift your emotional state. This typically looks like eating greasy food, sweet food, or over-indulging to make yourself feel better. According to Psychology Today, there are three levels of emotional eating. Situational, psychological, and biological.

Situational eating is when a circumstance influences your eating behaviors with two common factors of hunger and stress. Psychological eating is eating based on motivation or self-esteem. Restrained eaters think about food constantly, which is why they're more likely to indulge in emotional eating when feeling depressed or stressed. Compulsive eating is the tendency to eat without thinking. You eat just because you feel the urge to eat or you're bored and have nothing else to do. Biological eating is when you eat or don't eat based on how you view

your body. If you want to lose weight you may still indulge in food that's not good for you, and if you want to gain you'll do the same.

Overeating isn't the only indicator of stress, negative emotions or childhood trauma. Some people don't eat at all when they are stressed, so what's the difference? Are you eating because you're hungry, or is it a coping mechanism? When it comes to your childhood trauma, eating may have become your comfort food. Your scapegoat. Something that makes you forget about what's currently going on and helps you focus on anything else besides the trauma. How do you stop emotional eating? You can begin to practice time-management skills.

If you find yourself eating when you're bored or have free time on your hands, fill that time doing something productive instead.

You can start journaling, create a hobby, or start changing some of your negative habits into positive ones.

You can even begin effective problem-solving. The first step to effective problem solving is to understand the problem. You can do this by separating the facts from your feelings and focus on what can you do from where you are today. After you started the process of understanding the problem, you can begin

creating a plan for solving it. Lastly, you can execute the solution that you came up with. Look back at your experiences and ask yourself, "What could I have done better? How could I have responded?" This allows you to assess your mistakes and make adjustments so the same problems don't arise in the future. Even if they do, you'll properly be able to know how to solve it the second time around.

HOW TO MANAGE AND DEAL WITH YOUR EMOTIONS RELATING TO CHILDHOOD TRAUMA

There is no gain without struggle.
- Martin Luther King Jr.

If you want to stop the unhealthy habits of dissociation and emotional eating, then you need to tackle the triggers at their core. Your emotions. Emotions are fickle. They're up one minute, down the next. Remember, your feelings are learned behavior but your emotions amplify the feelings that you already feel. If you don't learn how to properly deal with your emotions as soon as they arrive, that's when you will be on what I call an "emotional rollercoaster." Emotions are habitual and generational. You handle your emotions ninety-nine percent of the time how you saw one of your parents handle theirs. You saw your mom holding grudges growing up and when you're left disappointed you find yourself holding a grudge too. If you saw your dad emotionally shut down growing up when you're faced with confrontation you shut down emotionally as well.

When we don't handle our emotions, our emotions evolve into our mood, and our moods then become our lifestyle.

We believe people are always negative or in a bad mood when it's actually habitual and generational emotions. When your emotions start to arise the first thing you need to do is breathe. I want you to do the five-second rule. Take five deep breaths for five seconds as soon as you start to feel any type of emotion. Whether that's anger, sadness, bitterness or anything else. When you begin to breathe you'll notice that your heart rate will go down and this will help decrease the anxiousness, anger, or sadness you feel immediately. Begin to focus on your body. When you're feeling these emotions ask yourself, "How is my body feeling? Is it tensing up? Is it sweating? Is it hot?"

This identifies what your trigger is. Physical sensation added to emotional sensations brings you to the realization of what your emotional and psychological triggers are. Once you've identified your triggers, ask yourself, "Do I feel like this as a result of my lack of boundaries? Am I allowing someone else to come into my space and trigger me?" If so, then creating better boundaries will help you with healing from your triggers. If not, then ask yourself, "What am I allowing? What am I willing to accept? What is non-negotiable?" When asking yourself these questions, ask them from the present version of yourself, not who you want to be in the future. Focus on who you are and what you want right now.

When you allow your emotions to rule you, you become extremely irrational and everyone becomes your enemy. It's important when facing your trauma and managing your emotions to continuously separate what is a fact to what is a feeling.

People behave based on how they feel about themselves, your family included.

Boundaries protect you and managing your emotions keep you grounded. When things go left, remember that you're still on the right path. To make sure you stay on track, here is a simplified guide on controlling your emotions. Remember the following:

1. *Your emotions determine your mood.*
2. *When you feel your emotions starting to overtake you, take five deep breaths for five minutes.*
3. *Analyze what you are feeling and why. This way, you know what triggers you.*
4. *Once you know your trigger, narrow in on it and identify if the reason is due to a lack of a boundary you didn't set.*

DOES YOUR CHILDHOOD TRAUMA CAUSE YOU TO SELF-SABOTAGE?

Self care is giving the world the best of you, instead of what's left of you. **- Katie Reed**

As we previously covered, setting boundaries around the people close to you is important. Setting a boundary on how you treat yourself is just as important. Has your childhood trauma caused you to self-sabotage? Behavior is said to be self-sabotaging when it creates problems in daily life and interferes with the goals that you have set for yourself. If you expect to see a change in your life without taking the time to do the work and create the mental space to change, then that's a result of self-sabotage. If you can't make decisions without the support of other people and need validation before you do something, you're self-sabotaging. If you hold onto negative thoughts that keep you from pursuing your dreams.

"I can't do this until I do that" somewhere in your childhood the ideation that you weren't enough presented itself. If you're constantly wasting your time doing things that are unimportant or constantly spins you around in circles.

31

Being in situations where you have the choice to be bitter or better, and you decide to be bitter, you choose the negative outcome to deal with your emotions.

Childhood trauma can cause us to over complicate problems, associating one detail not working as an entire project being broken, struggling to see the bigger picture. You begin to complain about everything, operating on imagination (how you think something is or how it should be) without facing the present reality of the situation. How do you stop self-sabotaging? Start focusing on one issue at a time. We all need to heal in one area or another, but we can't heal from ten different things at once. Find what is a pressing issue in your life. If you're reading this book it can be healing from childhood trauma or something else. Once you're healed you can begin the process of rebuilding your self-confidence and tackle the next issue that comes after. If you know you have certain behavior patterns, making an effort to change them is the first major step. Creating boundaries, giving yourself more space to heal, and doing more for yourself. For every negative thought or habit, write down two positive ways to combat it. This builds confidence and resilience.

HEALING FROM CHILDHOOD TRAUMA

Healing doesn't have to look magical or pretty. Real healing is hard, exhausting and draining. Let yourself go through it. Don't try to paint it as anything other than what it is. Be there for yourself with no judgement. **- Audrey Kitching**

Now that you went over the symptoms of childhood trauma and have identified yourself with some of them, it is time to begin the healing process. This chapter is the gut-wrenching chapter. The one that your trauma tells you to skip over, but you must take this chapter seriously. It will be the turning point in your healing. To begin, I want you to create a safe space. A space where you can be vulnerable and available to healing. We often expect our healing to process in one of two ways. Either overnight or we expect to never take our superhero cape off to show that we're actually in pain. This is your opportunity to be vulnerable, to be your true authentic self, and to begin the true healing process.

Before we go into the step-by-step process of healing, I want you to close your eyes and take a deep breath. When you begin to think about your trauma. Your heart may start to race. I want you and need for you to breathe. Now, the first step to

healing is to "Ground Your Trauma." What does it mean to ground your trauma? I want you to be present. I want you to be fully invested into right here, right now. I want you to shut everything off around you and be present.

Reliving trauma doesn't feel good, but as I said, true healing in the beginning never does.

Now that you're grounding the trauma, I need you now to "Recall The Trauma." This is the hard part. You may be like, "Well Dr. K I don't remember much of my childhood, how can I recall something I don't remember?" Do you remember that construction site we talked about, and the workers that are protecting you from the trauma? That's where your memory is, buried deep behind the wall that the workers are building. I would highly encourage you (if you don't remember the trauma) to seek a licensed professional who specializes in EMDR.

EMDR stands for Eye Movement Desensitization and Reprocessing. It's the process of bringing those buried memories to the forefront. If you do remember your trauma, even if it's vague, you can still recall your trauma. I want you to think back on what your parents told you, what your abuser did to you, and how the trauma made you feel. You can also flip this book to the opposite side to complete the healing exercise. On

34

one side of the exercise, I want you to write exactly what they did that hurt you. Whether that's sexual abuse, neglect, abandonment, whatever your trauma looks like, I want you to note the actions. On the other side, I want you to write exactly how the trauma made you feel. Whether it was how your parents yelling at you made you feel defenseless or how being sexually abused made you feel violated. On this list, remember that your childhood trauma does not have to be family. It can be being bullied in school or trauma at church. I want you to recall everything that was traumatic to you.

Now, I want you to "Sense The Trauma." I want you to be mindful of how your body is reacting to you recalling your trauma. Is your body tensing up? Are you getting hot? Are you beginning to sweat? If you're writing about how your dad left you and you begin to tense up, that's a trauma trigger. Take a deep breath, write out the trauma, and note how your body is feeling. If you have to cry, cry, if you want to scream, scream, if you want to be mad, be mad. Identifying how you feel is a vital part of healing. This doesn't mean be ruled by your emotions, instead, you are telling your emotions that you're taking back control.

Now it's time to "Love Your Trauma." Yes, I want you to love yourself. I want you to begin the processing of loving yourself so much to the point where you begin to release the responsibility of others in your life. You become mentally free when you begin the process of loving yourself. I want you to flip this book over and fill out the "What Are My Good Qualities?" sheet. I know this process is a lot. I know it's painful,

but if you don't heal from your trauma, your kids or your future kids will end up unconsciously carrying your trauma with them as we previously discussed. I know you don't want to carry this on to your future generations.

As I said, healing is not a one time fix. It is a process that you need to allow yourself to go through. Refer to these steps as often as you need.

1. *Ground your trauma. Remove every distraction and just be alone with yourself.*
2. *Recall the trauma. Go back to the place of trauma. If you begin to get triggered, remember to breathe.*
3. *Sense the trauma. Note how your body is reacting and write that down.*
4. *Love your trauma. You are more than what happened to you. Recognize all of the good qualities you have that make you, you.*

RELEARNING & REPARENTING YOUR CHILDHOOD TRAUMA

Daring to set boundaries is about having the courage to love ourselves, even when we risk disappointing others. **- Brene Brown**

After healing, comes the relearning process. I know that reparenting yourself can have a ton of backlash, but during this process, it's important to realize that your parents aren't always right. Reparenting means to heal from a childhood wound by making choices in your own best interest. The first step to re-parenting and relearning from your childhood trauma is to identify your beliefs. As we've previously discussed, your beliefs come from your childhood. Some beliefs are working hard to do something, the thought that you weren't born to be successful, that you can't conquer your dreams or anything else you believe.

What are you expecting? What do you want in life? What do you aspire to be like financially, emotionally, spiritually, mentally and physically? To become anything, you have to give up something. You cannot become without giving up a part of who you are now. If I want to stop becoming so consumed with my emotions, then I need to give up control. This also means I need to give up trying to control other people.

If you want to change you have to force it, you have to grab the reins of your life again and do what needs to be done.

There are three dimensions to reparenting and relearning: self-care, joy, and discipline. If you want to begin the reparenting process, you're going to have to focus on your physical body first. Our bodies are always speaking to us yet we don't pay attention. Keep practicing the art of having boundaries and remember that certain people cannot access certain parts of you anymore.

Boundaries are defined as the limits people set to create a healthy sense of personal space. Boundaries can be physical, mental, or emotional, they help distinguish the desires, needs, and preferences from one person to another. Before you can set boundaries you have to realize where you need to apply those boundaries. Boundaries need to be set when someone else's life, emotions, and problems, are personally affecting you. When you're consumed by everything they have going on, this can be a direct reflection of depression and anxiety.

I want you to ask yourself what the facts of the relationship are. We previously discussed the difference between facts and feelings. I want you to evaluate what is a fact in this rela-

tionship. I then want you to ask yourself how much can you give to the relationship without becoming emotionally and mentally drained. You can only overextend yourself so much to the point of reaching your breaking point and you need to do what's healthy for you. When we become an emotional dumpster for everyone's problems and neglect our own, we've become codependent on that relationship. When setting boundaries be brief and to the point. Often when we try to create boundaries we try to get the other person to understand how we feel and where we're coming from. This is the time to make your mental sanity a priority. Start with empathy by expressing how you feel. Try to avoid using the words "but" and "however." Instead of saying "I love you but...I hate when you do this" try saying things like "I love you and at the same time I need space." This allows you to express how you feel without trying to water down your boundaries.

When initially setting boundaries it's important for you to own your feelings. I'm not saying be ruled by them, I mean acknowledge that they exist. Instead of saying "I just feel like" say "I feel like you hurt me in this way." Boundaries can become ineffective when your tone isn't firm because when you don't honor yourself enough, you allow those boundaries to fade and you end up right where you started. For boundaries to be set in place, you need to put in the necessary work to keep them. You can have healthy boundaries with your parents. Healthy boundaries with your parents look like establishing what's off-limits to talk about, certain things you may not want to discuss and letting your parents know what is important.

Try to abstain from fixing your parent's problems. This sets a healthy boundary of no longer trying to be the parent in the relationship.

There are three different levels of boundaries you may fall into. Closed-off, middle ground, or healthy boundaries. Closed-off boundaries are when you avoid getting close with people, you don't ask for help, you hate rejection, you are detached, you are protective, and it doesn't take much for you to become jealous. Middle ground boundaries are when you involve yourself in everyone's issues, you are very dependent, you can't make decisions on your own, you have trouble telling people no, you accept disrespect, and you fear rejection. Healthy boundaries are when you do not compromise who you are to be in the presence of someone else, you're confident in your choices, you know your personal values, and you know what you're willing and not willing to accept.

The next step in reparenting and relearning from your childhood trauma is connecting with God. When you've experienced something deeply traumatic you're all over the place. It's important to have someone to center you. Find time to connect with God in a way that's realistic for you. This can be through reading your bible, listening to worship music, watching a church service on YouTube, whatever it looks like for you, do more of that.

This process is hard but completely doable. What I most want you to take away from the topic of reparenting is:

1. *The importance of identifying your beliefs. You may need to give up negative beliefs you have about yourself and pick up new ones.*

2. *Set a boundary as soon as you realize someone else's life is negatively affecting your own peace.*

3. *Separate facts from feelings. This will help you keep your boundaries in place.*

4. *Connect with something that will center you. Whether that be God, music or a hobby.*

To complete the relearning and reparenting process, flip to the back of this book to go through the belief exercise to help you identify what your beliefs are.

WAYS TO COPE, REPAIR OR RECOVER FROM A STRAINED RELATIONSHIP WITH A FAMILY MEMBER WHO HAS CAUSED YOUR CHILDHOOD TRAUMA

As I walked out the door toward the gate that would lead to my freedom, I knew if I didn't leave my bitterness and hatred behind, I'd still be in prison. **- Nelson Mandela**

Lastly, I want to help take you through the process of forgiving the family members who may be the direct cause of your trauma. The first step to any type of restoration with any family members is to first acknowledge the facts. We've been separating facts from feelings this entire book, now it's time to do it again. Regardless of what you deem as "right" or "wrong" let's look at the facts. Is the trauma you experienced generational? Is it you versus your dad, or is it you versus your great-great-great-grandfather? Did your parents know better, or were they just stuck in the generational cycle?

This is not excusing their behavior by any means, but this is getting you to see your trauma from a different lens. Did they attempt to connect back with you, restore the relationship, or apologize? If they did, then your pride is keeping you from

healing. If they didn't, then it's their pride keeping you from healing. Pride is like a plague. It spreads quicker than we can emotionally or mentally keep up with. How does your pride keep you from healing? Pride waits for closure when you don't need any. Pride waits for an apology when you know you're not going to get one. Family members who don't see anything wrong with their behavior won't take the initiative to restore things. That's why it's your responsibility as an adult to heal and forgive them for yourself. Let's start by communicating how you feel. Trauma can have you acting twelve years old trapped in an adult body, but the reality is you're not twelve, you're an adult. It's time to start communicating how you feel when you begin harboring resentment because resentment only hurts you, not them.

So how do you begin the forgiving process? Forgiveness is good for both your mental, emotional and physical health. Research shows that when we become better at forgiving we experience less stress, the tension in our body fades, and our levels of depression, anxiety, and anger drop. The first step to forgiveness is to first identify who you need to forgive and what pain they caused you. I want you to begin to acknowledge your emotions. I want you to ask yourself how you feel. Are you feeling sad? Are you feeling hopeless? Is it something more intense like guilt, disgust, or even hate? It may be difficult to recognize this feeling, but this is a pivotal part of healing. Forgiveness begins with you. It's not your fault why you've experienced the trauma, but it is your responsibility as an adult to heal from it.

To have the capacity to forgive others, you have to first forgive yourself for not knowing then what you know now.

We all learn and grow. Forgive yourself for some of the things you've personally done in the past. When going through the initial forgiving process, you have to work on your breathing. Breathe when you begin negative self-talk to yourself, or when you remember things that were said about you. The best revenge you could ever get is living your best life with no strings, no self-hate, or ill-willed attached. Stick to being present in the moment. Focus on healing today. Then when tomorrow comes, focus on healing tomorrow. Even though the pain is present, to repair, you can't simultaneously dwell on the past and rebuild the foundation for your future.

I want you to be free. I want to tell you how proud I am that you finished this book. You started this journey with me, unsure of what to expect. Yet you took it step by step and came out stronger for it. You may need to go back and refer to some of these chapters multiple times. And that's okay. Your process of healing looks like whatever it looks like. Whether it is long, ugly or frustrating, the truth is this is your story. The pen is in your hand, if you want it to be. I hope that with this pen, you

write the best story for yourself. I hope you write about how the workers who were building up a wall could finally go home. This wall they were building for so long got ordered to be torn down and so they did just that. The wall finally came down. Your wall crumbled.

Now you can finally rest.

TABLE OF CONTENTS

Be the kind of person that makes other people want to up their game.

www.theyoueffect.live

EMOTIONS JOURNAL

WHAT AM I FEELING?	WHY AM I FEELING LIKE THIS?

EMOTIONS JOURNAL

WHAT ARE THE FACTS?	WHAT ARE MY FEELINGS?

VICTIM TO VICTOR

WHAT DO I FEEL VICTIMIZED ABOUT?	HOW CAN I OVERCOME THIS?

HEALING EXERCISE

HOW DID THE PERSON THAT CAUSED YOU TRAUMA HURT YOU?	HOW DID THE TRAUMA MAKE YOU FEEL?

WHAT ARE MY QUALITIES?

10 THINGS THAT YOU LOVE ABOUT YOURSELF	10 THINGS THAT YOU WANT TO CHANGE ABOUT YOURSELF
1.	1.
2.	2.
3.	3.
4.	4.
5.	5.
6.	6.
7.	7.
8.	8.
9.	9.
10.	10.

IDENTIFY YOUR BELIEFS

What do I believe?	*Why do I believe this?*
Where did this belief come from?	*Do I still believe that this is true?*

What do I believe?	*Why do I believe this?*
Where did this belief come from?	*Do I still believe that this is true?*

IDENTIFY YOUR BELIEFS

What do I believe?

Where did this belief come from?

Why do I believe this?

Do I still believe that this is true?

What do I believe?

Where did this belief come from?

Why do I believe this?

Do I still believe that this is true?

IDENTIFY YOUR BELIEFS

What do I believe?

Why do I believe this?

Where did this belief come from?

Do I still believe that this is true?

What do I believe?

Why do I believe this?

Where did this belief come from?

Do I still believe that this is true?

IDENTIFY YOUR BELIEFS

What do I believe?	*Why do I believe this?*
Where did this belief come from?	*Do I still believe that this is true?*

What do I believe?	*Why do I believe this?*
Where did this belief come from?	*Do I still believe that this is true?*

IDENTIFY YOUR BELIEFS

What do I believe?	*Why do I believe this?*
Where did this belief come from?	*Do I still believe that this is true?*

What do I believe?	*Why do I believe this?*
Where did this belief come from?	*Do I still believe that this is true?*

INTENTIONS

www.theyoueffect.live

LIFE GOAL PLANNER
Projects and action steps to achieve my yearly goals.

TOP TWO ACTION STEPS TO GET ME THERE
1.

2.

TOP TWO ACTION STEPS TO GET ME THERE
1.

2.

TOP TWO ACTION STEPS TO GET ME THERE
1.

2.

TOP TWO ACTION STEPS TO GET ME THERE
1.

2.

TOP TWO ACTION STEPS TO GET ME THERE
1.

2.

MONTHLY
FINANCE TRACKER
Because money looks better in your bank account

www.theyoueffect.live

MY MONTHLY FINANCE TRACKER

Because money looks better in your bank account

Month of _____

DATE	INCOME AMOUNT	TRANSACTION DETAILS	DATE	INCOME AMOUNT	TRANSACTION DETAILS

Gross Income: **Total Expenses:**

MY MONTHLY FINANCE TRACKER

Because money looks better in your bank account

Month of _____

DATE	INCOME AMOUNT	TRANSACTION DETAILS	DATE	INCOME AMOUNT	TRANSACTION DETAILS

Gross Income: *Total Expenses:*

MY MONTHLY FINANCE TRACKER
Because money looks better in your bank account

Month of _____

DATE	INCOME AMOUNT	TRANSACTION DETAILS	DATE	INCOME AMOUNT	TRANSACTION DETAILS

Gross Income: *Total Expenses:*

Be The Game Changer.

www.theyoueffect.live

Productivity Chart (Before Month Starts)

	Rate: 1 as *Didn't Even Close*					10 as *Exceeded*				
Self-Love	1	2	3	4	5	6	7	8	9	10
Mindset	1	2	3	4	5	6	7	8	9	10
Childhood Trauma	1	2	3	4	5	6	7	8	9	10
Career	1	2	3	4	5	6	7	8	9	10
Goals	1	2	3	4	5	6	7	8	9	10

Score Directions: Add them and divide by 10.　　　**Score: _____/10**

Average is a 6-8.

Those in the 8-10 range typically are more focused, decisive and practice discipline and self control. Do you make decisions quickly and avoid analysis paralysis? Do you say no to anything not related to your monthy goals?

HOW TO IMPROVE YOUR PRODUCTIVITY CHART #?

Self-Love: How do you want to love yourself more this month?	**Mindset: How do you want to improve your thinking this month? What things do you say about yourself?**
Childhood Trauma: How is your child-hood trauma affecting you? How do you want to change?	Career/Goals: How well do you want to manage your time? How much of your to-do list do you want to accomplish everyday?

24

Productivity Chart (After Month Ends)

Rate: 1 as *Didn't Even Close*   10 as *Exceeded*

Self-Love	1	2	3	4	5	6	7	8	9	10
Mindset	1	2	3	4	5	6	7	8	9	10
Childhood Trauma	1	2	3	4	5	6	7	8	9	10
Career	1	2	3	4	5	6	7	8	9	10
Goals	1	2	3	4	5	6	7	8	9	10

Score Directions: Add them and divide by 10.   **Score: _____/10**

Average is a 6-8.

Those in the 8-10 range typically are more focused, decisive and practice discipline and self control. Do you make decisions quickly and avoid analysis paralysis? Do you say no to anything not related to your monthy goals?

HOW WELL DID YOU DO THIS MONTH?

Self-Love: What went well this month and what can you do to make next month even better?

Mindset: What did you say about yourself this month? How can you make it better for next month?

Childhood Trauma: How was this month for you? How can you make next month better?

Career/Goals: How well did you manage your time? How often did you stop for breaks? How much of your to-do list did you get done?

Productivity Chart (Before Month Starts)

Rate: 1 as *Didn't Even Close*   10 as *Exceeded*

Self-Love	1	2	3	4	5	6	7	8	9	10
Mindset	1	2	3	4	5	6	7	8	9	10
Childhood Trauma	1	2	3	4	5	6	7	8	9	10
Career	1	2	3	4	5	6	7	8	9	10
Goals	1	2	3	4	5	6	7	8	9	10

Score Directions: Add them and divide by 10.   **Score: _____/10**

Average is a 6-8.

Those in the 8-10 range typically are more focused, decisive and practice discipline and self control. Do you make decisions quickly and avoid analysis paralysis? Do you say no to anything not related to your monthy goals?

HOW TO IMPROVE YOUR PRODUCTIVITY CHART #?

Self-Love: How do you want to love yourself more this month?	**Mindset: How do you want to improve your thinking this month? What things do you say about yourself?**
Childhood Trauma: How is your childhood trauma affecting you? How do you want to change?	Career/Goals: How well do you want to manage your time? How much of your to-do list do you want to accomplish everyday?

Productivity Chart (After Month Ends)

Rate: 1 as ***Didn't Even Close***   10 as ***Exceeded***

Self-Love	1	2	3	4	5	6	7	8	9	10
Mindset	1	2	3	4	5	6	7	8	9	10
Childhood Trauma	1	2	3	4	5	6	7	8	9	10
Career	1	2	3	4	5	6	7	8	9	10
Goals	1	2	3	4	5	6	7	8	9	10

Score Directions: Add them and divide by 10.   **Score: ____/10**

Average is a 6-8.

Those in the 8-10 range typically are more focused, decisive and practice discipline and self control. Do you make decisions quickly and avoid analysis paralysis? Do you say no to anything not related to your monthy goals?

HOW WELL DID YOU DO THIS MONTH?

Self-Love: What went well this month and what can you do to make next month even better?	**Mindset: What did you say about yourself this month? How can you make it better for next month?**
Childhood Trauma: How was this month for you? How can you make next month better?	Career/Goals: How well did you manage your time? How often did you stop for breaks? How much of your to-do list did you get done?

Productivity Chart (Before Month Starts)

Rate: 1 as *Didn't Even Close*   10 as *Exceeded*

Self-Love	1	2	3	4	5	6	7	8	9	10
Mindset	1	2	3	4	5	6	7	8	9	10
Childhood Trauma	1	2	3	4	5	6	7	8	9	10
Career	1	2	3	4	5	6	7	8	9	10
Goals	1	2	3	4	5	6	7	8	9	10

Score Directions: Add them and divide by 10.

Score: ____/10

Average is a 6-8.

Those in the 8-10 range typically are more focused, decisive and practice discipline and self control. Do you make decisions quickly and avoid analysis paralysis? Do you say no to anything not related to your monthy goals?

HOW TO IMPROVE YOUR PRODUCTIVITY CHART #?

Self-Love: How do you want to love yourself more this month?	**Mindset: How do you want to improve your thinking this month? What things do you say about yourself?**
Childhood Trauma: How is your childhood trauma affecting you? How do you want to change?	Career/Goals: How well do you want to manage your time? How much of your to-do list do you want to accomplish everyday?

Productivity Chart (After Month Ends)

Rate: 1 as *Didn't Even Close*   10 as *Exceeded*

Self-Love	1	2	3	4	5	6	7	8	9	10
Mindset	1	2	3	4	5	6	7	8	9	10
Childhood Trauma	1	2	3	4	5	6	7	8	9	10
Career	1	2	3	4	5	6	7	8	9	10
Goals	1	2	3	4	5	6	7	8	9	10

Score Directions: Add them and divide by 10.   **Score: _____/10**

Average is a 6-8.

Those in the 8-10 range typically are more focused, decisive and practice discipline and self control. Do you make decisions quickly and avoid analysis paralysis? Do you say no to anything not related to your monthy goals?

HOW WELL DID YOU DO THIS MONTH?

Self-Love: What went well this month and what can you do to make next month even better?	**Mindset: What did you say about yourself this month? How can you make it better for next month?**
Childhood Trauma: How was this month for you? How can you make next month better?	Career/Goals: How well did you manage your time? How often did you stop for breaks? How much of your to-do list did you get done?

Happiness Chart (Before Month Starts)

Rate: 1 as *Didn't Even Close*   10 as *Exceeded*

Family Life	1	2	3	4	5	6	7	8	9	10
Career	1	2	3	4	5	6	7	8	9	10
Frienships	1	2	3	4	5	6	7	8	9	10
Day to Day	1	2	3	4	5	6	7	8	9	10
Health	1	2	3	4	5	6	7	8	9	10

Score Directions: Add them and divide by 10.   **Score: _____/10**

Average is a 6-8.
Those in the 8-10 range typically wake up happy. Do you wake up happy and excited to start the day?

HOW TO IMPROVE YOUR HAPPINESS CHART #?

What are some things that you want to do to improve your overall happiness?

How will you take control of your happiness this month?

How will you show yourself self-care this month?

Happiness Chart (After Month Ends)

	Rate: 1 as *Didn't Even Close*						10 as *Exceeded*			
Family Life	1	2	3	4	5	6	7	8	9	10
Career	1	2	3	4	5	6	7	8	9	10
Frienships	1	2	3	4	5	6	7	8	9	10
Day to Day	1	2	3	4	5	6	7	8	9	10
Health	1	2	3	4	5	6	7	8	9	10

Score Directions: Add them and divide by 10.   **Score: _____/10**

Average is a 6-8.
Those in the 8-10 range typically wake up happy. Do you wake up happy and excited to start the day?

HOW TO IMPROVE YOUR HAPPINESS CHART #?

What are some things that you did to improve your overall happiness this month?

How did you take control of your happiness this month?

How did you show yourself self-care this month?

Happiness Chart (Before Month Starts)

Rate: 1 as *Didn't Even Close*   10 as *Exceeded*

Family Life	1	2	3	4	5	6	7	8	9	10
Career	1	2	3	4	5	6	7	8	9	10
Frienships	1	2	3	4	5	6	7	8	9	10
Day to Day	1	2	3	4	5	6	7	8	9	10
Health	1	2	3	4	5	6	7	8	9	10

Score Directions: Add them and divide by 10.   **Score: _____/10**

Average is a 6-8.
Those in the 8-10 range typically wake up happy. Do you wake up happy and excited to start the day?

HOW TO IMPROVE YOUR HAPPINESS CHART #?

What are some things that you want to do to improve your overall happiness?

How will you take control of your happiness this month?

How will you show yourself self-care this month?

Happiness Chart (After Month Ends)

Rate: 1 as *Didn't Even Close*   10 as *Exceeded*

	1	2	3	4	5	6	7	8	9	10
Family Life	1	2	3	4	5	6	7	8	9	10
Career	1	2	3	4	5	6	7	8	9	10
Frienships	1	2	3	4	5	6	7	8	9	10
Day to Day	1	2	3	4	5	6	7	8	9	10
Health	1	2	3	4	5	6	7	8	9	10

Score Directions: Add them and divide by 10.   **Score: _____/10**

Average is a 6-8.
Those in the 8-10 range typically wake up happy. Do you wake up happy and excited to start the day?

HOW TO IMPROVE YOUR HAPPINESS CHART #?

What are some things that you did to improve your overall happiness this month?

How did you take control of your happiness this month?

How did you show yourself self-care this month?

Happiness Chart (Before Month Starts)

	Rate: 1 as *Didn't Even Close*						10 as *Exceeded*			
Family Life	1	2	3	4	5	6	7	8	9	10
Career	1	2	3	4	5	6	7	8	9	10
Frienships	1	2	3	4	5	6	7	8	9	10
Day to Day	1	2	3	4	5	6	7	8	9	10
Health	1	2	3	4	5	6	7	8	9	10

Score Directions: Add them and divide by 10.   **Score: _____/10**

Average is a 6-8.
Those in the 8-10 range typically wake up happy. Do you wake up happy and excited to start the day?

HOW TO IMPROVE YOUR HAPPINESS CHART #?

What are some things that you want to do to improve your overall happiness?

How will you take control of your happiness this month?

How will you show yourself self-care this month?

Happiness Chart (After Month Ends)

	Rate: 1 as *Didn't Even Close*						10 as *Exceeded*			
Family Life	1	2	3	4	5	6	7	8	9	10
Career	1	2	3	4	5	6	7	8	9	10
Frienships	1	2	3	4	5	6	7	8	9	10
Day to Day	1	2	3	4	5	6	7	8	9	10
Health	1	2	3	4	5	6	7	8	9	10

Score Directions: Add them and divide by 10.   **Score: _____/10**

Average is a 6-8.
Those in the 8-10 range typically wake up happy. Do you wake up happy and excited to start the day?

HOW TO IMPROVE YOUR HAPPINESS CHART #?

What are some things that you did to improve your overall happiness this month?

How did you take control of your happiness this month?

How did you show yourself self-care this month?

MONTHLY CHECK-IN

WHAT WAS GREAT ABOUT THIS MONTH?

WHAT DID I LEARN THIS MONTH?

**HOW WELL DID I MANAGE THIS MONTH?
HOW CAN I BE BETTER?**

**WHAT CHALLENGED ME THIS MONTH THAT I CAN
GROW FROM?**

WHAT AREAS OF MY LIFE NEED IMPROVEMENT?

MONTHLY CHECK-IN

DID I HAVE FUN THIS MONTH? WHAT WOULD I NEED TO DO TO ENJOY MYSELF MORE?

HOW MANY TIMES DID I TAKE TIME TO REWARD MYSELF THIS MONTH?

HOW MANY TIMES DID I TAKE TIME TO MYSELF THIS MONTH?

The best way out is through.

www.theyoueffect.live

HEALING
Journal Prompts

www.theyoueffect.live

What impact has the experience of childhood trauma had on your life as an adult?

What feelings did you have as a child toward the person who caused your trauma?

THE YOU EFFECT

How did the abuse or neglect or abandonment make
you feel about yourself as a child?

*How do you feel about yourself as an adult now with
the pain you've experienced as a child?*

_____

_____

_____

_____

_____

_____

_____

_____

_____

_____

_____

_____

_____

_____

_____

_____

_____

_____

_____

_____

_____

_____

_____

_____

What are your present feelings toward the person who's caused your abuse?

How do you currently feel about forgiveness?

Why are you choosing forgiveness?

_____

_____

_____

_____

_____

_____

_____

_____

_____

_____

_____

_____

_____

_____

_____

_____

_____

_____

_____

_____

_____

_____

_____

_____

Write a letter of your feelings, be as real as possible. release all the emotions you've kept bottled up.

Dear _____

_____

_____

_____

_____

_____

_____

_____

_____

_____

_____

_____

_____

_____

_____

_____

_____

_____

_____

_____

_____

_____

_____

_____

_____

What decisions have you let others make for you?
List 10 of them.

1.

2.

3.

4.

5.

6.

7.

8.

9.

10.

What decisions will you make for yourself?
List 10 of them.

1.

2.

3.

4.

5.

6.

7.

8.

9.

10.

5.

_____

4.

_____

3.

_____

2.

_____

1.

_____

List 5 things you will tell yourself that will make you more confident when you make decisions.

THE YOU EFFECT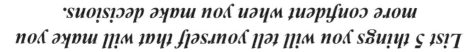

Evaluate the people that are currently in life, do you feel loved and accepted by them? If not, what would make you feel loved and accepted? What could you do? What could they do?

Do you feel as if your accomplishments are recognized? If not, how can you advocate for yourself more?

Do you feel listened to, understood, or heard? If not, how can you speak up for yourself more? How can you express yourself more assertively?

Do you feel as if the people you're in a relationship with (whether family, friends, or romantic) treat you with respect? If no, how can you establish firmer boundaries with them?

Are you hard on yourself? If yes, how can you show yourself more grace?

Describe circumstances in your life that caused you to be disappointed in other people. Have you put your trust more in people than yourself?

Describe circumstances and situations in your life that has caused you to feel like a failure. Have you been so hard on yourself, that you forgot to acknowledge your progress?

_____

_____

_____

_____

_____

_____

_____

_____

_____

_____

_____

_____

_____

_____

_____

_____

_____

_____

_____

_____

_____

_____

_____

_____

What family, friends, or partners have caused you to feel abandoned? Have you struggled with finding your inner voice and trusting it?

List actions that you can take that will help you stop being so codependent and lean into being independent.

Losing someone is not easy. Describe the feelings you experienced when you learned the loss of the person you love?
*Please note that if someone has left your life, but they're not

physicallly dead that still counts as a loss*

_____

_____

_____

_____

_____

_____

_____

_____

_____

_____

_____

_____

_____

_____

_____

_____

_____

_____

_____

_____

_____

_____

_____

What are some positive things you miss about the person you lost?

List 3 things you hope to accomplish today.

THE YOU EFFECT

List 3 things you did accomplish today.

5.

_____

4.

_____

3.

_____

2.

_____

1.

_____

List 5 things that you value about yourself.

THE YOU EFFECT

List 3 top things you want to change about yourself.

How has trauma influenced your work, family, personal relationships, your mental, emotional, and physical health?

In what ways has this made you more closed off, or more resistant to letting people in? In what ways has this made you stronger?

_____
_____
_____
_____
_____
_____
_____
_____
_____
_____
_____
_____
_____
_____
_____
_____
_____
_____
_____
_____
_____
_____
_____
_____
_____

How has the trauma affected how you make decisions?

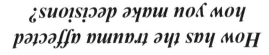

*Write about the positive decisions
you have made thus far.*

Where are you today? What areas of your life are causing you the most emotional pain?

What emotional needs are you trying to receive from someone else?

What unmet needs are you experiencing that you don't believe that you can fulfill yourself?

_____
_____
_____
_____
_____
_____
_____
_____
_____
_____
_____
_____
_____
_____
_____
_____
_____
_____
_____
_____
_____
_____
_____
_____
_____

What stops you from living the life you've always wanted to live?

Write a list of every negative thing you can think of that you tell yourself.

Write a list of a positive trait to combat all the negative traits you listed this morning. For every negative one, write two positive traits.

Write a letter to your younger self.
What advice would you give yourself?

Dear Self,

_____

_____

_____

_____

_____

_____

_____

_____

_____

_____

_____

_____

_____

_____

_____

_____

_____

_____

_____

_____

_____

_____

_____

Now using the advice you gave yourself, how can you apply that to who you are today?

Write a list of the people you need to forgive.

Write 3-4 sentences to each person to why you need to forgive them and what you need to forgive them for.

_____
_____
_____
_____
_____
_____
_____
_____
_____
_____
_____
_____
_____
_____
_____
_____
_____
_____
_____
_____
_____
_____
_____
_____

When I'm emotionally or mentally drained, the best thing I can do for myself is...

THE YOU EFFECT

_____
_____
_____
_____
_____
_____
_____
_____
_____
_____
_____
_____
_____
_____
_____
_____
_____
_____
_____
_____
_____
_____
_____
_____
_____
_____

How can I show myself more self-love?

What boundaries do you need to have in your life?

How much can you give in the relationship that you need to set boundaries with, without going mentally insane?

What are you tolerating that's draining you?

What problems are you taking on that's not yours?

Are you allowing people to come into your space and negatively affect you, your emotions, and your mental health?

_____

_____

_____

_____

_____

_____

_____

_____

_____

_____

_____

_____

_____

_____

_____

_____

_____

_____

_____

_____

_____

_____

_____

_____

_____

*What are you willing to accept? What is
non-negotiable in a relationship for you?*

**What are some lies about yourself
that childhood trauma has told you?**

_____

_____

_____

_____

_____

_____

_____

_____

_____

_____

_____

_____

_____

_____

_____

_____

_____

_____

_____

_____

_____

_____

_____

_____

_____

_____

Do you believe the lies that childhood trauma has told you to still be true? If yes, why?

What are you trying to protect yourself from?
Why do you feel this way?

Do you find yourself overly sensitive to criticism?
If yes, why?

Do you need contant reassurance from other people? If yes, why do you need this?

Do you often feel insecure and unworthy?
Do you feel as if everything is your fault?

Do you find it hard to trust people?

Do you often suppress your feelings? If yes, do you overthink? What are some of the thoughts you have?

_____
_____
_____
_____
_____
_____
_____
_____
_____
_____
_____
_____
_____
_____
_____
_____
_____
_____
_____
_____
_____
_____
_____

(ruled lines)

Do you go out of your way to avoid confrontation?

THE YOU EFFECT

Do you become easily attached to people? Even emotionally unavailable and toxic people?

_____

_____

_____

_____

_____

_____

_____

_____

_____

_____

_____

_____

_____

_____

_____

_____

_____

_____

_____

_____

_____

_____

_____

_____

_____

Do you try to please other people?
Do you blame yourself a lot?

THE YOU EFFECT

Do you have a pattern of staying in unhealthy relationships?

What are you doing in order to please your parents even though it isn't working well for you?

Whta do you need to do for yourself, even if your parents disapprove?

What boundaries do you need with your parents?

What is one step you can take toward setting those boundaries?

THE YOU EFFECT

How do you try to change or "fix" your parents?
How do you feel when you fail to change them?

*With regards to your relationship with your parents,
what is in your control?*

What feels safe to share with your parents?

_____

_____

_____

_____

_____

_____

_____

_____

_____

_____

_____

_____

_____

_____

_____

_____

_____

_____

_____

_____

_____

_____

_____

_____

_____

_____

_____

What doesn't feel safe to share with your parents?

How does your parent exploit your kindness by expecting you to meet their demands 24/7?

_____

_____

_____

_____

_____

_____

_____

_____

_____

_____

_____

_____

_____

_____

_____

_____

_____

_____

_____

_____

_____

_____

_____

_____

_____

HEALING JOURNAL PROMPTS

Can you release some of the guilt you feel by remembering that you're setting healthy boundaries and taking care of yourself just as other adults do?

How do you feel?

What do you need right now? How can you give yourself more of what you need?

What can you say "no" to today?

What did you say "yes" to today?

What is your purpose in life?

_____

_____

_____

_____

_____

_____

_____

_____

_____

_____

_____

_____

_____

_____

_____

_____

_____

_____

_____

_____

_____

_____

_____

_____

_____

_____

_____

What are your biggest aspirations in life?

**What thoughts are you thinking
that's polluting your mind?**

What are the things in your life that are consistent?
What makes them consistent?

What are the things in your life that are inconsistent?
What makes them inconsistent?

_____

_____

_____

_____

_____

_____

_____

_____

_____

_____

_____

_____

_____

_____

_____

_____

_____

_____

_____

_____

_____

_____

_____

_____

_____

What in your life distracts you?

What in your life keeps you going?

*What questions about yourself have you left
unanswered? Why have you left them unanswered?*

Are you doing the work that matters?
If not, what's stopping you?

List 10 of your bad habits.

1. _____

2. _____

3. _____

4. _____

5. _____

6. _____

7. _____

8. _____

9. _____

10. _____

THE YOU EFFECT

List 10 things you're going to do to change them.

1. _____

2. _____

3. _____

4. _____

5. _____

6. _____

7. _____

8. _____

9. _____

10. _____

What in your life feels out of your control?

How can you regain control of your life?

What triggers your anger?

How can you control your anger?

What triggers your anxiety?

What causes you to be in a depressive state?

What conflict can you avoid?

_____

_____

_____

_____

_____

_____

_____

_____

_____

_____

_____

_____

_____

_____

_____

_____

_____

_____

_____

_____

_____

_____

_____

_____

_____

_____

What parts of your life are driven by your trauma?

_____

_____

_____

_____

_____

_____

_____

_____

_____

_____

_____

_____

_____

_____

_____

_____

_____

_____

_____

_____

_____

_____

_____

What situations has caused you, your peace?

What boundaries do you need to set to protect your peace?

List 5 ways you can listen to your inner voice more.

1.

2.

3.

4.

5.

By not listening to your inner voice, how are you making things harder on yourself?

What happiness are you putting off?

How do you compromise your happiness?

What would your life be like if you focused on the present moment?

What can you do today to say "yes" to your dreams?

What dreams did you say "yes" to?

THE YOU EFFECT

What can you pay closer attention to today?

How can you take better control of your emotions?

_____

_____

_____

_____

_____

_____

_____

_____

_____

_____

_____

_____

_____

_____

_____

_____

_____

_____

_____

_____

_____

_____

_____

_____

Are you self-aware, self-sabotaging, or self-critical?

**How can you become more self-aware,
less sabotaging, and less critical?**

Do you have trouble forgiving yourself?

THE YOU EFFECT

How can you forgive yourself more?

Does your actions reflect your character?
Are you pleased or displeased?

_____

_____

_____

_____

_____

_____

_____

_____

_____

_____

_____

_____

_____

_____

_____

_____

_____

_____

_____

_____

_____

_____

_____

_____

_____

Why do you have a deep desire to please other people?

How often are you taken for granted? How can you change this? What needs to be put into place?

How do you see yourself?

_____

_____

_____

_____

_____

_____

_____

_____

_____

_____

_____

_____

_____

_____

_____

_____

_____

_____

_____

_____

_____

_____

_____

_____

_____

How can you change how you see yourself?

How often do you talk negative to yourself?

How does talking negative change how you view yourself? How do you feel when you do it?

_____
_____
_____
_____
_____
_____
_____
_____
_____
_____
_____
_____
_____
_____
_____
_____
_____
_____
_____
_____
_____
_____
_____
_____
_____

How do you respond during an argument?

How has the way you respond affected your relationships?

**What are you currently feeling? What are the facts?
What are your feelings?**

THE YOU EFFECT

How are you feeling now? How did fact checking your feelings feel?

158

Evaluate your friends.
List their names & their qualities.

Do you feel like you overgive in friendships? How can you change this?

Who do you look up to? Why?

How does the person you look up to help you in everyday life?

_____

_____

_____

_____

_____

_____

_____

_____

_____

_____

_____

_____

_____

_____

_____

_____

_____

_____

_____

_____

_____

_____

How have you sold yourself short?

How can you regain confidence to stand firm in your everyday life?

What is happening in THIS present moment?
(as you write this)

List out your wins for today.
(whether big or small)

_____

_____

_____

_____

_____

_____

_____

_____

_____

_____

_____

_____

_____

_____

_____

_____

_____

_____

_____

_____

_____

_____

_____

_____

Are there any feelings or memories you have been supressing today, last week or in the past years?

List out any emotions you want to express, but haven't.

Do you know your triggers? Have you expressed what your triggers are to others?

Have you identified what makes you at peace?
This is just as important as knowing
what triggers you.

**What can you do today that your
future self will thank you for?**

What personal milestones do you want to accomplish within the next six months?

_____

_____

_____

_____

_____

_____

_____

_____

_____

_____

_____

_____

_____

_____

_____

_____

_____

_____

_____

_____

_____

_____

_____

_____

_____

_____

What qualities do you think make up a best friend?
Loyalty, honesty, open mindedness?

Are you the friend you seek or desire in other people?

*Admitting that you have fears is part of personal growth.
Is there a fear you have that no one else knows about?*

_____

_____

_____

_____

_____

_____

_____

_____

_____

_____

_____

_____

_____

_____

_____

_____

_____

_____

_____

_____

_____

_____

_____

_____

_____

Are you able to narrow down where these fears come from?

What life decisions have you been avoiding? There could be a decision from years past or just this week.

Courage is being scared and doing what needs to be done anyway. What will you say yes to that may require some extra courage?

Do you consider it difficult for you to build connections with others? If so, why?

What made it easy for you to connect with the people you are close to presently?

Are you replacing one thing for another? Example: Are you replacing a friendship to fill the void of a past relationship?

Do you see a pattern or cycle where you replace one relationship for another?

What is going well in your life today?

Is there anything you would have done differently about your yesterday, like greet or react differently?

_____

_____

_____

_____

_____

_____

_____

_____

_____

_____

_____

_____

_____

_____

_____

_____

_____

_____

_____

_____

_____

_____

_____

_____

_____

_____

_____

_____

What does your morning routine look like? Do you want to make any changes to it?

_____

_____

_____

_____

_____

_____

_____

_____

_____

_____

_____

_____

_____

_____

_____

_____

_____

_____

_____

_____

_____

_____

_____

_____

_____

What is your night time routine? Is there anything you would like to add or remove from your nightly routine?

What is a pesonal goal you would like to set for today?

Did you reach your goal? If so, how did achieving that goal make you feel? If not, are you willing to try again tomorrow?

What negative thoughts have you been giving the most attention to?

What positive thoughts can you use in place of the negative ones?

*Concerning your future, what
are you most scared about?*

Write down how you can start planning so you do not have those fears.

_____

_____

_____

_____

_____

_____

_____

_____

_____

_____

_____

_____

_____

_____

_____

_____

_____

_____

_____

_____

_____

_____

_____

_____

_____

*When life does not seem to go
your way, how do you react?*

What do you tell youself when things do not go your way? Do you feel like giving up or are you able to brush it off and keep going?

If someone is saying something negative, how does it usually affect you? Do you become negative too?

Do you find it hard to stay in a positive mindset?

THE YOU EFFECT

When faced with a challenge, do you imagine a positive outcome or a negative one?

When something good happens to you, do you tend to think it can't last or are you able to enjoy it?

When thinking about the person who was involved in your childhood trauma, which emotions do you feel most strongly?

_____
_____
_____
_____
_____
_____
_____
_____
_____
_____
_____
_____
_____
_____
_____
_____
_____
_____
_____
_____
_____
_____
_____
_____

How do you respond when someone hurts you now?

THE YOU EFFECT

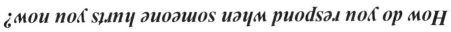

What are you most looking forward to tomorrow?

How fulfilling was your day yesterday? Better than expected?
What was in your control that could have made it better?

How do you treat the people you love? Do you shower them with gifts and offer support?

How do you treat yourself? Do you give yourself the same treatment?

What are you proud of yourself for?

Is there anything that continues to cause you to feel ashamed?

Is there any area in which your childhood trauma made you stronger? Do you feel it has only made you weaker instead?

If you could choose one mood to be in all day, which would it be? Grateful, happy, humorous, etc.

What stopped you from being in that mood all day?
Did something come up to frustrate you?

Describe your favorite childhood memory. Go in depth with details like what season it was and who was there.

What makes this your favorite memory?

_____

_____

_____

_____

_____

_____

_____

_____

_____

_____

_____

_____

_____

_____

_____

_____

_____

_____

_____

_____

_____

_____

_____

_____

_____

What have you learned about what triggers you?

THE YOU EFFECT

What did you discover was hardest to separate facts from feelings? Was it topics relating to relationships, or something more?

THE YOU EFFECT

In what area do you feel you haved healed most in?

☁☀

Which lesson, habit, routine or tip about childhood trauma do you most want to make sure you continue?

_____

_____

_____

_____

_____

_____

_____

_____

_____

_____

_____

_____

_____

_____

_____

_____

_____

_____

_____

_____

_____

_____

_____

What improvements have you seen in yourself most?

_____

_____

_____

_____

_____

_____

_____

_____

_____

_____

_____

_____

_____

_____

_____

_____

_____

_____

_____

_____

_____

_____

_____

_____

How far do you think you have come to setting healthy boundaries? Do you feel like you have taken steps in the right direction?

THE YOU EFFECT

*Out of all the advice given, what
was easiest for you to implement?*

Out of all the advice given, what has been the hardest to implement?

_____
_____
_____
_____
_____
_____
_____
_____
_____
_____
_____
_____
_____
_____
_____
_____
_____
_____
_____
_____
_____
_____
_____
_____
_____

CPSIA information can be obtained
at www.ICGtesting.com
Printed in the USA
FFHW021809111019
55526970-61320FF

9 781087 808451